SPANISH MISSION

HASTINGS

STYLES OF FIVE DECADES

This book is one in the series
THE COSMOS COLLECTION
concerning the Architectural Heritage
of New Zealand.

Other books at present in the series or
in course of preparation include

ART DECO NAPIER—STYLES OF THE THIRTIES
First Edition published Reed Methuen 1987
Second Edition published Cosmos Publications 1990

NELSON—CITY WITH A HERITAGE
To be published 1992

WHITESTONE OAMARU
To be published 1992

SPANISH MISSION

HASTINGS

STYLES OF FIVE DECADES

Peter Shaw and Peter Hallett

☆☆☆ COSMOS ☆☆☆

COSMOS PUBLICATIONS – PO BOX 5153 NAPIER – NZ

First Published in 1991 by

COSMOS PUBLICATIONS
PO Box 5153, NAPIER, NEW ZEALAND

with the assistance of Hastings District Council

National Library of New Zealand
Cataloguing-in-Publication data

Shaw, Peter, 1946-
  Spanish Mission Hastings : styles of five decades / Peter Shaw
and Peter Hallett. Napier, N.Z. : Cosmos, 1991
  1 v.
  ISBN 0908887051 (pbk.)
  ISBN 0908887043 (hbk.)
  1. Architecture--New Zealand--Hastings. 2. Architecture--New
Zealand--Havelock North. I. Hallett, Peter, 1922-
II. Title. III. Title: Hastings.
  720.9933

ISBN 0 908887 04 3 (hard cover)

ISBN 0 908887 05 1 (soft cover)

ACKNOWLEDGEMENTS

In writing and photographing this companion to our **Art Deco Napier – Style of the Thirties**, we have cause to be grateful once again to the many Hawke's Bay residents who permitted us access to their homes and business premises.

We are again indebted to Robert McGregor, Deputy Director of the Hawke's Bay Museum and President of the Art Deco Trust Inc., for his interest, support and generosity with both time and information.

James Morgan, Editor of the Hawke's Bay Herald Tribune, June Johnson of the Havelock North Public Library and Joan McCracken at the Alexander Turnbull Library, Wellington, all gave invaluable assistance.

Julia Grigg spent dusty hours among the old building permits held by the Hastings District Council. We greatly appreciate her tenacity as a researcher.

Susan Hallett and Patrick Sherratt contributed vitally at all stages of the writing and photographing of this book.

We gratefully acknowledge the support and encouragement we have received from the Mayor, Mr Jeremy Dwyer and members of the Hastings District Council. In many ways this book is an acknowledgement of the Council's far-sighted decision to promote the city's distinctive architectural character.

Peter Shaw
Peter Hallett
1991

HAWKE'S BAY HERALD TRIBUNE

SPANISH MISSION
HASTINGS
STYLES OF FIVE DECADES

In 1929 Lovell and Painter, Printers of Queen Street, Hastings were responsible for the production of a copiously illustrated 'Official Handbook of Hastings for Tourist, Sportsman and Settler'. Initiated by the then Hastings Borough Council it was designed to draw visitors to a town which at this time was less well known than its nearby and older neighbour, Napier.

Taking a grandly omniscient view, the Handbook's opening pages emphasised the beauties of Hawke's Bay in a style which, although quaint by today's standards, nevertheless captured the essence of the place. It referred to the province's noble stretches of hills, to its blossoming orchard lands, to the vivid blueness of its river waters. Then, moving to Hastings' site in the Heretaunga Plains, it described the myriad streams which join the three rivers, Ngaruroro, Tukituki and Tutaekuri "... as they flow from the mountains to unite with a naturally fertile soil and a climate which the pagans would have thought was made according to the formula of their goddess of the harvest to make the district an ideal home for man and beast, and for everything that good land, water and sunshine can bestow."

The writer of this purple prose does not mention the fact that the former Maori owners, members of the Ngati Kahungunu tribe, had appreciated the qualities of the Heretaunga Plains long before the Pakeha ever set foot on it. Although the swampy plains were not inhabited in pre-European times, they were a valuable source of food as well as flax and raupo, both useful for clothing and as building material.

It was these Maori inhabitants who, imagining a partnership of equal benefit to both races, initially encouraged the Pakeha to settle in central Hawke's Bay during the 1850s. They were adamant that the Heretaunga Plains remain in Maori ownership. As relations between the two races deteriorated following the outbreak of the Maori-Pakeha Land Wars in other parts of New Zealand, the Maori gradually became less willing to sell their land to settlers whose motives they now began to suspect. Finally in 1870 under circumstances of dubious legality the Heretaunga Plains passed out of Maori ownership. They did so as the price paid for peace in Hawke's Bay.

In 1867 a group of settlers led by Thomas Tanner was able first to lease and then in 1870 to purchase a total of 19,385 acres. Historian Mary Boyd called the Heretaunga Purchase "the most notorious example of a new method of direct purchase by private individuals introduced by the Government in 1865 to overcome Maori resistance to land-selling." In the following years, despite fears of war and outright confiscation of Maori land, a Maori Repudiationist Movement fought to have the disputed purchase declared fraudulent and overturned. It was unsuccessful.

The town of Hastings had its origin in the piece of land known by the Maori name of Karamu. It was here that a railway station was built in 1873 on the line from Napier to Pakipaki. The land was officially owned by one Francis Hicks, who had earlier purchased a 100-acre block from Thomas Tanner. Despite a persistent local legend, it is unlikely that it was ever named Hicksville; instead the town commemorates Warren Hastings, the first British Governor-General of India, and thus it continued the imperial colonial associations which had already led to the naming of Napier, Clive and Havelock.

In 1873 a town plan was produced for an auction of sections which began on July 8th. The first day of the sale concluded with a champagne evening put on by Francis Hicks. Settlers returned the following day to bid even more keenly for property. The swamps were drained, the flax, scrub and fern burned off to create pasture. Now a grid-like pattern was imposed on it and streets given names which recalled the English origins of the settlers. Sales continued through the following decade as the original landowners were forced to subdivide by an increasingly unfavourable economic climate.

Unlike Napier, which because of its location quickly took on the appearance of an English seaside resort, Hastings developed during the 1870s and 1880s as a service town for its extensive rural hinterland. By 1882 the population of Hastings numbered 617 and there were 131 freehold landowners living in the growing town. The greatest period of expansion took place after

Stoneycroft, one of the earliest surviving 2-storied villas in the area, was built for W. Birch of the Erewhon Station on the Taihape Hills as a convenient town house.

1885 when Hastings rapidly developed a modest commercial area around its railway station.

Architecturally, it had the appearance of many similarly sized New Zealand settler towns. Houses in the cottage or villa styles were built in wood supplied by the firm of Knight Brothers which had opened in 1876. By far the most substantial of these was the enormous two storeyed veranda-ed villa built at Riverslea by Thomas Tanner. A Post Office, Fire Station, and the Hastings District School all followed as did an Anglican wooden church of St Matthew which welcomed its first congregation in 1877 to a Gothic styled building whose facade bore a distinct resemblance to the West Front of Westminster Abbey.

During the following two decades many businesses were established. Hotels with promenading verandahs were built, the most commodious being the Hastings Hotel, designed by the Napier architect W.A. Dugleby, who duplicated dining and sitting rooms in the interests of class demarcation. The Albert Hotel which also dates from this period, is the only survivor. A Town Hall, more churches, and banks in the classical style favoured for such buildings at the time followed. They were mostly the work of builders who understood wood and whose designs reflected the fashionable styles of the day. Because most of early Hastings was built in wood it is not surprising that few original buildings survive today. In February 1893 a particularly serious fire destroyed much of the town's central business district.

It was not until the turn of the century that architects began to work in Hastings, by which time there were citizens wealthy enough to afford the services of such professionals. One of the first was George Sollitt (1834-1912) a Yorkshireman who set up practice in Hastings in 1890 from Christchurch where he had been a general contractor since his arrival at Lyttelton on board the Lady Jocelyn in 1879. He shrewdly perceived that the services of an architect would be required by wealthy landed Hawke's Bay settlers either anxious to upgrade their original dwellings or to build new homes on smaller land holdings in the wake of the Seddon government's imposition of a land tax which made larger holdings uneconomical. Sollitt soon established the flourishing architectural practice of Sollitt and Allan.

Sollitt's Church of the Sacred Heart in Heretaunga Street remains today as prominent as it was in 1895 when it was built at a cost of £3300. It replaced a much smaller church, designed by Dugleby, which now survives as a schoolroom. Its foundation stone was laid by Archbishop Redwood on 7 October 1894. Compared with "Westminster Abbey" built nearly twenty years earlier, Sacred Heart is even more soaringly Gothic. Its central spire is

The wooden St Matthew's Anglican Church (1877) whose facade was deliberately built to resemble the West Front of Westminster Abbey.

JOHN MURTAGH COLLECTION, HASTINGS

The Albert Hotel as it is today.

supported by pointed corner buttresses and provided with pinnacles; its interior detailing shows that Sollitt was an expert in designing in wood, a skill which was to prove useful in attracting clients wishing to use his services as a domestic architect.

Two of his large houses survive today while a third, Waiterenui, although altered in the 1920s, still bears signs of his expertise. In 1899 he designed an enormously extended single-storeyed wooden villa at Horonui for H.M. Campbell, a newly married wealthy man in his early twenties whose sociable personality no doubt determined his decision to incorporate a magnificent rimu-panelled billiard room and servants quarters to accommodate a permanent staff of six. Horonui, a house built on land originally a part of the much larger Poukawa station established by his father, is distinguished by a verandah stretching along the length of the house which gives panoramic views down a long valley towards the distant Hastings.

The following year Sollitt designed Greenhill, at Raukawa Road, for Archibald McLean. Originally part of the huge Maraekakaho Station established between 1852 and 1873 by Sir Donald McLean but later subdivided, Greenhill was spectacularly sited on a hill overlooking the Ngatarawa Plains whose 19,000 acres had been purchased from the Maori during the 1860s. The architect, no doubt inspired both by the site and his client's aspiration to be lord of all he surveyed, designed a three-storeyed central viewing turret which dominates the villa. No expense was spared. On a verandah frequently interrupted by porticos, paired posts are elaborately turned; shingled gables adorn a roof structure of enormous complexity; eaves are supported by brackets of widely varying types. Although fireplaces, mouldings and stained glass windows are more ornate than at Horonui, where the comparative restraint is certainly more elegant, Greenhill remains a unique example of High Victorian wooden domestic architecture in New Zealand.

Also working in Hawke's Bay at this time was Charles Tilleard Natusch (1859-1952) who had established a practice in Wellington in 1886 following his emigration from England. The architectural office which he bought at Napier from Robert Lamb continues to this day with one of C.T. Natusch's grandsons, Guy, as its senior partner. Like Sollitt, Natusch was devoted to wood. He became well known for large houses built in what is usually referred to as an Elizabethan style because it owes much to the fashion for Tudor domestic revivalist building in England during the latter years of the nineteenth century. Natusch was quick to appreciate its applicability in New Zealand, where there were abundant supplies of hardwood suitable for building.

St Andrew's Presbyterian Church (1906) was designed by C.T.Natusch in his favourite half-timbered Elizabethan manner.

ALEXANDER TURNBULL LIBRARY
Auckland Star Collection

10

At Matapiro his client was Walter Shrimpton, another early landowner who in 1872 had arrived in Hawke's Bay as a land valuer. In 1875 he and a partner purchased 22,000 acres of land from its previous Pakeha owners, and built a single-storeyed house on a terrace near an old Ngati Upokoiri whare whakairo (carved meeting house). In 1902 he decided to engage C.T. Natusch to transform this house into a homestead, a process which took eight years to complete.

The result was a large emphatically symmetrical two-storeyed house with separate half-timbered gables on either side of deep verandahs which served both storeys. Like both Horonui and Greenhill, its timber frame is clad with rusticated weatherboards, its roof is of corrugated iron. Timber ornamentation is much more restrained than on Sollitt's houses, reflecting a more modern approach to decoration, as the Art Nouveau stained glass windows above the magnificent staircase and on fanlights in sitting and bedrooms indicate.

Sollitt adopted the more old-fashioned view that quantity of detail is paramount, while Natusch preferred to please the eye by carefully varying the spacing of his verandah balustrading and keeping ornament to a minimum. His layout of the interior, while providing many formal rooms of generous proportions, is notable for its profusion of corridors, those for service functions being narrow and dark, while others for family use are wider and less gloomy. Approached by a long drive Matapiro is still surrounded by the superb gardens for which it has long been famous in the area.

C.T. Natusch in partnership with F.H. Frankland was also responsible in 1912 for a huge house called Tunanui. This property of 30,000 acres had been taken up by Captain Andrew Russell, who with his brother William had first come to New Zealand in 1857 as a member of the 58th Regiment. The 1912 house was built for Sir Andrew Hamilton Russell, who, following service with the British Army in India, had come to farm in New Zealand in 1892.

Tuna Nui is a timber-framed house set on concrete foundations, clad not in weatherboards but in two-inch thick stucco, with a Marseilles tiled roof. For insulation its interior walls are lined with powdered pumice on cedar slats, a procedure unusual in New Zealand but relatively common in the United States. The rather surprising use both of this technique and of stucco by an architect well known for his allegiance to wood owes much to the fact that F.H. Frankland had been an architectural engineer in the U.S. before coming to New Zealand. The hand of C.T. Natusch is more clearly evident in the hall of this massive two-storeyed house; it is rimu panelled and conceived on an even grander scale than that at Matapiro.

The Cliff Press Building and the Cotterill &Humphries Building designed by J.A.Louis Hay of Napier in 1915. Both are typical of the unstrengthened brick buildings which crumbled during the 1931 earthquake.
ALEXANDER TURNBULL LIBRARY

Queen Street in the mid-1920's.
JOHN MURTAGH COLLECTION, HASTINGS

The Grand Hotel designed by C.A.Vautier, Hawke's Bay's highest building of the times, did not survive the earthquake.
ALEXANDER TURNBULL LIBRARY
Auckland Star Collection

The impressive 1909 Hastings Post Office designed by John Campbell, the Government Architect.
ALEXANDER TURNBULL LIBRARY
Lovell Smith Collection

Tuna Nui is one of the first buildings in the Hastings area to depart significantly from the standard wooden villa type of domestic architecture found in towns all over New Zealand. Hastings had many such houses, the 1913 Mudgway House built by architects J.A. Grant and J. Ball at 800 Duke Street being a particularly fine example.

In the centre of the town a number of large buildings were constructed in brick and plaster rather than wood. Of these one of the most notable was the Grand Hotel designed by another local architect, C.A. Vautier, in a highly eclectic Edwardian Baroque manner. Few of Hastings' timber hotels had managed to survive the fires with which the town was all too often plagued. In these years no one imagined that the Grand or the 1909 Post Office, one of the most imposing designed by the Government Architect, John Campbell, would have to contend with an earthquake as massive of the one which destroyed them both in 1931. It is even more ironic that the city's last surviving brick Edwardian Baroque building, Penty and Lawrence's 1914 Union Bank of Australia, having survived the earthquake, was demolished by its owners the ANZ Bank as late as 1984.

A new St Matthew's Anglican Church, built to designs by C.J. Mountfort of Christchurch on the site of the old "Westminster Abbey" and consecrated in 1886 had been considerably extended in 1914. The addition of a chancel, Lady chapel, transept and tower built in an unusual variation of the original church's wooden Gothic was by Wellington architect Frederick de Jersey Clere. Its unpainted ferro-concrete construction supported by octagonal piers instead of buttresses may have given it a forbidding appearance but certainly ensured its survival in the earthquake. The church formerly possessed a higher tower which was lowered in 1931.

Noteworthy inside St Matthew's is the work of the eminent English stained glass artist Karl Parsons (1884-1934), whose 1914 five-light 'Adoration of the Blessed Virgin with Christ, Shepherds and the Magi' dominates the chancel. In 1926 Parsons made three additional windows for the Lady Chapel, each of them characterised by sumptuous colours, a highly worked surface and beauty of design. It is said that these owe their particular intensity of colour not only to his skill and his reaction to seeing the medieval windows at Chartres Cathedral in 1924 but also to his understanding of the constant level of bright Hawke's Bay sunlight which would illuminate his glowing forms.

The Napier architect J.A. Louis Hay (1881-1948) also did some work in Hastings in this period and his brick office premises for Cotterill and Humphries in 1915, which did not survive in 1931, are an early example of the influence of the work of the great American architect Frank Lloyd Wright.

Earlier, Hay, who had spent his apprenticeship years from 1896 serving articles in the Natusch office, designed wooden houses very much in the manner of his masters. Though not a thorough Domestic Revivalist he nevertheless seems to have favoured half-timbered gables on his otherwise conventional early villas. Like many architects familiar with ideas of domestic comfort illustrated in the English 'Studio' magazine in the first decade of the new century, he frequently specified the use of Art Nouveau stained glass windows and was fond of giving sitting rooms inglenook fireplaces. ·

In 1912 he designed a huge concrete house for Selwyn Chambers in the hills above Havelock North. Called Kopanga, it was built, unusually, in solid concrete and thus sustained only minor damage in the earthquake. Hay, struck by the panoramic views across the Heretaunga Plains, designed a north facing facade with deep verandahs and groups of large double-hung sash windows; the projecting verandah balustrades in concrete derive from C.T. Natusch's wooden ones but look clumsy by comparison. The upper storey's flattened central gable with its wide overhanging eaves already indicates Hay's familiarity with the Californian bungalow.

Plans and elevations of bungalows had been regularly appearing in New Zealand's 'Building Progress' magazine and were eagerly seized upon by architects looking for a way to escape the omnipresent villa. Kopanga shows that Hay, working on a large commission for a wealthy client, was prepared to try something new but was not yet able to dismiss his familiar way of working.

His even more massive Te Mahanga, designed for John Douglas in 1918, was constructed in brick and plaster and consequently collapsed entirely in 1931. Contemporary photographs reveal a house with a lower storey of plastered roughcast but a Natusch-like upper storey complete with half-timbered gables and long sleeping verandahs.

These latter two features, in addition to the tiled roof and turret-room, were highly fashionable in the Hastings-Havelock area at the time as the work of another architect clearly shows.

The prolific Hastings architect William Rush (1872-1965) was to use these features in creating a regional Hawke's Bay style. Born at Northhampton where he was articled to an architectural firm, he arrived in New Zealand in 1904 and in 1906 formed a partnership with E.T. James which lasted until 1914. This partnership, so the magazine 'Progress' informed its readers in April 1911, "may be relied upon to give that artistic touch which makes a home of a house." Their most prominent buildings today are Havelock North's Village Hall (1911) and

Virginia creeper soon covered Frederick de Jersey Clere's 1914 concrete additions to the original wooden St Matthew's Church designed in 1886 by C.J.Mountfort.
ALEXANDER TURNBULL LIBRARY
Radcliffe Collection

Front and rear views of the house Te Mahanga which Louis Hay designed in 1918.
LOUIS HAY ALBUM

W.J.Rush's HOME FOR THE SIMPLE LIFE and
HAWKE'S BAY COUNTRY HOUSE The plans were
published in The Forerunner in 1911 and 1913, but neither
of these houses was ever built.

HAVELOCK NORTH LIBRARY

the nearby St. Luke's Church (1912).

Attracted by the sunny climate, it was Rush who was the first of many Hawke's Bay architects to envisage the appropriateness of the Spanish Mission style to the region. He began tentatively, realising that it would be unwise for a new architect to contradict a prevailing fashion for Domestic Revivalism, but gradually he introduced elements of a Californian style which in time became acceptable to his clients.

The combination of features from both English Domestic Revival and Californian styles can best be seen on his own 1908 House at the top of Durham Drive, Havelock North. Called Ngawiwi, the Maori word used to translate his own surname, the house has villa-like squared bay windows with multi-paned fanlights above. The eaves of its main half-timbered gable project out in the fashionable Californian manner; the rows of pointed exposed rafter ends underneath were also fashionable at the time and much used by Louis Hay. The house has a number of sleeping verandahs either of the more modern Californian Spanish arcaded variety, made in stucco, or balustraded with elaborately cut posts. During the two years that Rush and his family lived in this house the architect was suffering from tuberculosis and one of the main reasons for his advocacy of the sleeping verandah from that time on was his adherence to the fashionable medical opinion that the condition of those with weak lungs would be helped by sleeping out of doors.

A competent watercolour painter and illustrator, he submitted plans and elevations to 'The Forerunner', the magazine published by Havelock residents interested in fostering discussion of religious, scientific and educational questions. In the edition for January 1911 he illustrated and wrote 'A Home for the Simple Life', advocating deep verandahs for sleeping and dressing as well as al fresco dining beneath wisteria-draped pergolas. Because his aim was to promote an outdoor lifestyle it is not surprising that the Californian style with arcaded verandahs and wide overhanging eaves should be deemed appropriate. His 'Hawke's Bay Country House' in 'The Forerunner' of December 1913, planned around a courtyard, also has these features.

Neither of these bungalows was ever built, clients tending to favour something more conventional such as the two-storeyed McHardy House (1916), though it too was provided with a Californian verandah gable above its upper storey sleeping verandah. A circular turreted open garden room forms an unexpected conclusion to the ground floor's verandah which stretches along the front of the house. Rush liked the effect of cream painted stucco walls, orange Marseilles tiled roofs and green painted window trim.

His work was not limited to domestic building. In 1911 for Woodford House at Havelock North he decided on an appropriately English model. Instead of the traditional Gothic school, he designed a building characterised by wide-angled, downward sweeping rooflines broken with dormer windows much in the manner of C.F.A. Voysey. Sloping chimney forms accentuated the resemblance while half-timbered gables acknowledged the fashionable English Domestic Revival. Again the walls were stuccoed and the elegant rooflines tiled. The timbered Hall with its scissor-trussed rafters is manorial; classrooms and the Dining Room were timber panelled to head height, their ceilings displaying heavy beams. Rush's school building at Woodford House cleverly succeeded in emphasising a domestic rather than an institutional character.

In 1913 he also designed Heretaunga School, now called Hereworth, and the more innovative Iona College. Iona still exhibits the Spanish Mission character which Rush gave it in 1913 which the architect Edmund Anscombe fully respected in his restoration of the school's buildings after they were seriously weakened following the earthquake. It is interesting that Rush was working on Iona in the same period as Atkinson and Abbott designed what remains New Zealand's largest and most impressive building in the Spanish Mission style, Auckland Grammar School.

Iona's arcaded cloisters recall those of the Spanish Missions of California; the main building's central tower has round-headed windows reminiscent of Mission belltowers; overhanging eaves are supported on ornamental brackets which, like Auckland Grammar's, owe something to the Californian Craftsman bungalow style also popular at this time. Typically Spanish too is a balcony with a set of three windows above the library's sun-trap bow window. The three windows have rounded fanlights and are separated by the characteristic barley twist columns which were later to become such a common feature on Hastings' post earthquake buildings. A comparison of photographs of the original buildings with those taken after the 1931 restoration reveals that these windows and columns are not the work of Rush and James but of Edmund Anscombe who, in adding a storey above the original bow window-ed library in 1931, added to Iona's Spanish Mission character details which were to re-appear on his 1932 department store for Westerman Brothers in Heretaunga Street.

No survey of the architecture of this area would be complete without mention of the Havelock North houses of J.W. Chapman-Taylor (1878-1958). This architect came to Havelock North in 1913 three years after having returned from England where he had visited some of the main protagonists of the Arts and Crafts movement. Like Rush, Chapman-Taylor saw the possibility of

An early photograph of Woodford House as it looked soon after the completion of the buildings designed by Rush in 1911.

ALEXANDER TURNBULL LIBRARY

The Spanish-influenced buildings at Iona College by Rush in their original form, dating from 1913.

ALEXANDER TURNBULL LIBRARY
Radcliffe Collection

Iona photographed in 1931 during the course of the restoration work undertaken by Edmund Anscombe.

ALEXANDER TURNBULL LIBRARY

The Rest House, Havelock North designed by
J.W.Chapman-Taylor in 1915. Originally a competition
design commissioned by the Havelock North Town Board,
the building later housed the transformer which first
brought electricity to the area.

HAVELOCK NORTH LIBRARY

adapting English architectural ideas to the New Zealand climate.

The circumstances which led him to move from Wellington to Havelock and to build a number of houses there are unusual. In 1908 a Hastings businessman, Reginald Gardiner, gathered a group of prominent local citizens to read and discuss literary matters. Gradually they developed this into a highly active cultural society called The Havelock Work specifically to encourage performances of music and drama. It was these people who produced 'The Forerunner', the magazine to which both Rush and Chapman-Taylor were occasional contributors. The same people were responsible for raising money by organising an Old English Village Fete in 1911 and a Shakespearian Pageant in 1912 to finance the building of Havelock's Village Hall.

Both Reginald Gardiner and his wife Ruth were interested in meditation as a means of gathering wisdom about the spiritual and philosophical truths which lay behind the more formalised religion of the various Christian churches. In 1910 a visiting priest from the Anglican monastic order, The Community of the Resurrection, became acquainted with the Havelock Work's interests and it was through him in 1912 that Dr Robert William Felkin arrived in Havelock North.

This remarkable man was a graduate of both Edinburgh and Heidelburg universities. Inspired by a childhood meeting with Dr David Livingstone he became an explorer who travelled widely in Africa and was reputed to be the first man accurately to measure the Pigmy people of the Congo. He was also a pioneer student of tropical diseases, a staunch Anglican and a tireless student of esoteric spiritual knowledge. For the small Havelock community which Reginald Gardiner had gathered around him, Dr Felkin's presence was inspirational. During the three months which he spent in the town of less than five hundred inhabitants he established a branch of the London-based hermetic Order of the Golden Dawn, called 'Stella Matutina' (Morning Star). He gave the Havelock chapter the name of 'Smaragdum Thalasses' (Emerald Seas) and initiated its first adherents to the order's secret rituals before returning to England. By 1916, encouraged in the belief that the climate in Hawke's Bay would be good for his now failing health, Dr Felkin returned to Havelock with his second wife Harriot and Ethelwyn, his daughter by a previous marriage. He set up practice as a general practitioner and, until his death in 1926, supervised the order he had founded.

Before they left New Zealand, Dr Felkin and his wife had been generously provided with a piece of land below his own property at Tauroa by Mason Chambers. The architect appointed was Chapman-Taylor who then came from Wellington with his own family to work in Havelock. The house, called Whare

Ra, is unusual because here the architect was to some extent obliged to depart from his Arts and Crafts principles in order to accommodate his client's specifically religio-philosophical as well as architectural requirements.

It is oriented along an east-west axis because this is the same direction as Moses had cast his tent. Beneath the house is a large rectangular concrete basement which houses the Temple, the eastern end of which culminates in a seven-sided vault whose walls, doors and ceiling are to this day still covered with brightly coloured astrological, kabbalistic and other symbols.

On its upper level the plastered brick, roughcast-finished house looks more conventional. Much less obviously English than Chapman-Taylor's other houses of this period, it has the deep verandahs so common in Hastings and Havelock houses. Its flattened gables give the exterior of the house a Californian appearance but inside Arts and Crafts hand-adzed woodwork door fittings, exposed jarrah beams and a baronial fireplace all indicate that Chapman-Taylor was given the opportunity to demonstrate his affection for the hand-crafted medievalising features to which he was always devoted. The house was divided into a family living area, at the southern end, which had its own entrance and was joined by a corridor leading to bedrooms and eventually to the more formal drawing room from which the order's robed adherents were led blindfolded down a circuitous staircase to an antechamber connected to the Temple.

One particularly innovative aspect of the design was the architect's ingenious solution to the problem of darkness in rooms behind a deep verandah. By operating sliding panels, light entered the rooms through glass tiles which were placed in the roof. So that Dr Felkin's consulting rooms could be situated close by, William Rush designed an annexe to Whare Ra, which was later removed and now sits at the bottom of the drive which leads up to the house.

In 1917 the house called Turama (Lantern) which Chapman-Taylor had designed in 1916 for Reginald Gardiner was built in Duart Road, just below Whare Ra. Turama is perhaps less unusual as an example of Chapman-Taylor's work though it is more extensively decorated in carved Christian and Rosicrucian symbols than Whare Ra. From the evidence of an article extolling the importance of ritual in revealing inner truth which Chapman-Taylor contributed to 'The Forerunner' in 1912, he too was a member of the inner circle which gathered around Dr Felkin and Reginald Gardiner.

In 1919 Chapman-Taylor built Oak Trees, which he described as "a workshop fitted as a temporary dwelling" in Campbell Street as a home for his family while he built Sunborne on a section just above it in Duart Road,

Havelock. The larger house is distinguished by an open garden room which the architect had not originally designed but added during the course of construction. Its floor is a reinforced concrete slab and the walls an extraordinary honeycomb construction of empty petrol cans set between layers of reinforced concrete.

Like Rush and others concerned with The Havelock Work and its associated spiritual quests, Chapman-Taylor believed that people should live in close association with the outdoors. He planned his own house so that sun and fresh air could enter all its interior spaces. The plan also emphasised the importance of close-knit family social functions; dining, sitting by the fire or, in summer, in the garden room. The inglenook around the fireplace bore a motto "O ye fire and heat, bless ye the Lord, praise him and magnify Him forever."

The other eminent New Zealand architect to work in the Havelock area was W.H. Gummer (1884-1966). His association with the wealthy landowning Chambers family came about as the result of his friendship with Maurice Chambers who from 1919 to 1926 lived at Louis Hay's Kopanga. Maurice's wife was Miriama Chambers (nee Batley) the sister of Te Oira Arani Batley, who married W.H. Gummer whom she had first met at Tauroa while still a pupil at Woodford House. The close association between Gummer and members of the Chambers family was to result in his building four magnificent houses between 1916 and 1935.

The first, Tauroa, dates from 1916 and was built for Mason and Madge Chambers as a replacement for their wooden house which had burned to the ground in 1914. From the first, Mason Chambers determined on an earthquake and fireproof home and immediately engaged Gummer, already a highly rated young architect with experience in the London office of Sir Edwin Lutyens and that of Daniel Burnham in Chicago. On returning to New Zealand in 1913 Gummer had become the Auckland partner in the Wellington-based firm of Hoggard and Prouse. The correspondence between the architect and his client reveals that in 1914 Gummer produced at least three different plans for the new Tauroa which, in 1916, was eventually built with double brick walls with a cavity between. Reinforced ferro-concrete pillars and beams added to the strength of the house which was finished in white stucco. Timber is either jarrah, because of its slow burning properties, or kauri.

Tauroa is one of New Zealand's most distinguished houses. In plan it is adventurous; all of its rooms radiate along two axes from a point at the base of a staircase which sweeps up on both sides of a circular hall. This plan also determines the unusual proportions of some of the rooms which back on to the hall. The dining room, for instance, has a curved wall which necessitated the designing of special furniture. Again the relationship between inside and outside was exploited, many of Tauroa's rooms opening either on to pergolas or verandahs. The local fetish for sleeping outside seems not to have been confined to clients of Louis Hay and William Rush.

Individual touches of craftsmanship are everywhere. The owner's initials are emblazoned on the finger plates of door furniture; in the dining room a beaten copper hood above the fireplace carries a Latin inscription: "Benedicite ignis et aestus domino, laudate et super exaltate cum in secula" which translates as "Bless fire and warmth in the name of the Lord. Praise and exalt Him on high for ever."

This inscription is remarkably similar to the motto which adorned Chapman-Taylor's fireplace, a coincidence no doubt explainable by the fact that both men were closely associated with Dr Robert Felkin and his Order.

It is significant that the houses designed by Rush, Gummer, and Chapman-Taylor for members of the Order of the Golden Dawn closely reflected the spiritual concerns of their clients. For both, an interest in the relationship between the physical and the metaphysical went hand in hand with a respect for truth to materials and the values of honest craftsmanship. The philosophical concerns of Mason Chambers, Reginald Gardiner and other followers of Dr Felkin had precise architectural counterparts in these doctrines of the Arts and Crafts movement. Tauroa owes much to an English Arts and Crafts-derived devotion to fine workmanship. Local craftsmen hand-wrought the jarrah bannister as well as its ornate iron supports. In the dining room tiny bronze figurines appear to slide down the light cords; the library's floor-to-ceiling bookcases have specially designed shelves which slope outward to form convenient reading surfaces.

Tauroa also demonstrates the transition between its architect's allegiance to English Arts and Crafts models and the Beaux Arts classicism which was to become so evident in his commercial buildings of the 1920s. His favourite fasces motif decorates the ceiling in the library; a Doric frieze defines the dado in the music room; the motif of a circle within a square is found at the tops of doors; the cornice of the dining room ceiling consists of bands of dentils. Gummer's growing preference for restrained classically-derived detailing is everywhere apparent. The extensive glazed area of the hall contains clear leaded glass panels rather than the colourful floral Art Nouveau arabesques to which Louis Hay, for instance, remained devoted until the geometries of Frank Lloyd Wright's stained glass work made their inevitable impact on his decorative

Guests leaving after a garden party at Tauroa in 1923.
HAWKE'S BAY MUSEUM

work.

Efficiency rather than craftsmanship led to the provision of a centralised vacuum cleaning system at Tauroa but this piece of domestic sophistication never operated because the ship transporting its electric motor was sunk during its wartime voyage to New Zealand.

The exterior of Tauroa is equally extraordinary. Its many shuttered windows give it a Georgian appearance while the upper storey balconies refer to the persistent Californian Spanish influence which was already becoming such a pronounced feature of the regional architecture of Hastings and Havelock. In a touch that is pure Spanish Mission, there is even an aperture designed to house a small bell in the wall of one of the wings. Distinctly modern for the time is the house's flat roof, obscured behind outlined parapets of varying heights.

Gummer's next Hawke's Bay house, originally called Craggy Range but now known as Belmount, was built between 1918 and 1919 for William Van Asch who had purchased a part of the Tukituki Station in 1913. Although certain aspects of the house's design remained unresolved upon its completion, Craggy Range represents its architect's earliest attempt to produce something which owed less to specific historical styles than to the modern English architecture with which he became familiar during his years of travel between 1908-1913.

Craggy Range's geometric rigour shows that Gummer must have been familiar with the 1908 house called Upmeads designed by Edgar Wood, an English architect who was initially the leading Arts and Crafts architect in the north of England but who by 1908 was one of the so-called English Free School. He had experimented with "uncraftsman-like" concrete, as did Chapman-Taylor and Gummer in New Zealand.

Both Upmeads and Craggy Range are exposed brick houses but Gummer chose to reveal his use of concrete by means of a string course to mark the distinction between the two storeys and in the heavy garden frontage with arcaded concrete balcony above. This overbearing feature upsets the proportions of the cubic forms which are otherwise such a distinctive feature of all elevations. Like both Wood and Lutyens, Gummer used a great variety of sizes of metal-framed windows, irregularly disposed over the facades. Again, as at Tauroa, the flat roof is hidden by a shallow parapet which steps up and down as the roof line varies. Like Tauroa the service area at the rear of the house is angled out and away from its main elevation and there is the same profusion of balconies and oddly shaped chimneys.

Inside Craggy Range the modernistic austerity of design persists. The dining room's brick fireplace is severely geometric; the billiard room is lined with exposed brick, the hall and library with Queensland maple; the staircase which ascends in the centre of the house has an unusually large number of turns and the first landing has a seat set into the wall to permit a moment of rest during the ascent.

Craggy Range was exceptional for its time, there being no New Zealand precedent for its unashamedly modern appearance. Gummer's English sources are clear; it is likely that, having travelled in the USA in 1913, he was familiar with contemporary Californian domestic architecture which was moving away from the excesses of Spanish Mission to something more restrainedly geometric. Belmount has never received the attention it deserves, probably because of its remote though magnificent location looking straight at Te Mata Peak across the Tukituki Valley.

Gummer's two later Hawke's Bay houses, Arden (1926) and Te Mata (1935) were built for members of the Chambers family. Arden, originally the home of Maurice and Miriama Chambers, is an elegant composition built of reinforced concrete and brickwork with a plaster finish. Interior joinery is totara. In conception the house exhibits many similarities with Spanish Modern houses in California, which combined a restrained use of Spanish features with a more pared back approach to detailing. Both Gummer and C.R. Ford, his partner since 1923 in what was already by 1926 New Zealand's premier architectural practice, had travelled in California. Ford spent the first six months of 1923 there on what his passport described as a "study and observation" tour. The photograph album he assembled on his return indicates an intense enthusiasm for modern Spanish Mission-influenced domestic architecture—not for the over-decorated buildings of the first decade of the century but for the work of contemporary architects whose interests lay in much more subtle allusions to California's Mission background.

The drawings for Arden indicate that the design concept was Gummer's and that the structural solutions involved were in the capable hands of C.R. Ford. Also involved was the practice's senior draughtsman, Gordon Wilson. He had been employed by Hoggard, Prouse and Gummer since 1918, was to become a partner at Gummer and Ford in 1928 and, later still, the New Zealand Government Architect.

Arden's symmetrical facade is characterised by a group of round-headed, fan-lit French doors; above, an open balcony leads back to covered verandahs off bedrooms. The house's west facing elevation incorporates an exterior staircase leading up to the flat roof upon which it was once intended to build a swimming pool. There is also an elegant little Juliet balcony. Like its predecessors, the detailing of Arden was given a distinctive unifying geometric motif which is best seen on the upper portion of the garden facade but is also used extensively inside, notably on the balusters of the main staircase. The porte cochère Gummer designed in 1926 was not built until 1985 when the house's owners used the architect's plans to complete this important feature of his original conception.

The restraint with which Gummer and Ford incorporated a number of Spanish Mission features is characteristic of their work. By contrast William Rush's 1920 design for Te Mata, Bernard Chambers' house which crumbled to the ground in the 1931 earthquake, was fussily insistent in its heavy handed reference to a Spanish Mission style which had long since been superseded in both California and New Zealand.

From the architect's surviving watercolour elevations it is clear that Rush's huge stuccoed brick house sported the whole range of arcaded balconies, verandahs and doorways, groups of windows with bracketed hoods, parapeted gables as well as a brick-outlined bull's-eye window and an oriel window. Early photographs show that some of the arcaded verandah openings were able to be shaded with canvas blinds designed to protect sleepers from being awoken by early morning sun. Rush seems to have adopted a policy of including as many features as possible on his facades; the result of such an assemblage of references to Spanish Mission style was a house lacking any sense of unity.

However, unity was something which Gummer and Ford emphatically provided their client with in 1935 when a new Te Mata was built. While the exterior's shuttered windows and tiled roof continued the Californian Spanish influence, interior planning and detailing are more conventionally neo-Georgian in approach. There are considerable asymmetries in its irregular arrangement of windows, porches and balconies; verandahs are now supported on slim wooden square columns and a balcony decorated with a wooden lattice balustrade. Generally, restraint is the hallmark of Gummer and Ford's Te Mata. There is an impressive entrance hall at the centre of the house containing a staircase and large patterned clear glass windows.

Rooms are disposed in the formal Georgian manner on either side of the central hall; downstairs rooms lead directly from one to the next while upstairs they are entered along corridors on either side of a landing at the top of the stairs. The Queensland maple panelling in the dining room, door surrounds in maple or walnut and an arched set of double doors, formerly the entry to Rush's Te Mata, were re-used from the earlier house. As usual, the highest standards of craftsmanship characterise every aspect of the new Te Mata's construction.

Gummer's private houses for a landed elite were relatively inaccessible to the public and remain so today. In Hastings itself it was rare to find buildings of such extravagance though after 1907 when the breakup of the Pepper Estate occurred some fine houses were built in the vicinity of Duke, York and Fitzroy Streets. In York Street Rush designed a large two-storeyed house for the Newbigen family in 1912. In 1914 an unknown architect was employed to design the Cato House for a client who had seen a picture of an English house in a book and wanted to have something similar built in Hastings. Called St Brigid's, the house is unusual in having a sun-trap plan, something which Chapman-Taylor had also used a number of times already. In the same year the young Hastings architect Albert Garnett (1878-1956) designed the Beatson House in York Street using the now familiar English model Rush had popularised. In 1911 and 1914 respectively he proved that he was prepared to desert this model in favour of the single-storeyed Californian bungalow when he produced the large homesteads Torran and Glen Aros in Raukawa Road for landowners occupying sections of what was formerly McLean's Maraekakaho Estate.

Garnett's career lasted well into the mid 1950's. Although details of his training are unknown, he was assisted in his rise to early prominence by being the eldest son of James Garnett, a well known builder in the area who had been elected Mayor of Hastings in 1911. Between 1921 and 1924 Albert Garnett himself was a member of the Hastings Borough Council. Later, in partnership with Harold Davies and Eric Phillips, Garnett was a member of the town's most reputable and prolific architectural practice.

In 1912 he designed a new Methodist church in what the 'Hastings Standard' described as "an indifferent style of Gothic," but there were greater things in store for him. In 1911 his father, during his term as mayor, negotiated the purchase of land on the corners of Heretaunga and Eastbourne Streets on which the council proposed to build a municipal building, shops, offices and a theatre. By 1914 the town was ready to proceed and the architect Henry Eli White (1877-1952), already eminent in Wellington for his 1912 St James Theatre and soon to become known throughout Australasia as an innovative theatre designer, was appointed to carry out the design. White was ultimately to design only the Municipal Theatre in Hastings. A competition was held for the design of the Municipal Buildings but only architects practising within three miles of the Hastings Post Office were invited to submit proposals. This effectively excluded any Napier architects from entering the competition. From

The Hastings Methodist Church, designed in what was described as "an indifferent style of Gothic" by Albert Garnett in 1912.
ALEXANDER TURNBULL LIBRARY

the eight submissions Albert Garnett was chosen as winner by the judge, Wellington architect Joshua Charlesworth.

White's Municipal Theatre was built first. To this day it remains Hastings' largest and most significant Spanish Mission building and one of New Zealand's finest theatres. The St James in Wellington is an opulent Edwardian Baroque structure; his masterpiece, Sydney's State Theatre was to be Gothic in inspiration. The Hastings Municipal Theatre has a Spanish Mission exterior but is lavishly decorated inside with motifs which indicate White's familiarity with the work of continental Art Nouveau architects and designers, particularly the Austrian Secessionist Josef Maria Olbrich who designed the highly influential 1897-88 Secession House in Vienna.

For Henry Eli White consistency of exterior and interior style was not an issue. His theatres were to be lavishly decorated palaces of entertainment rather than architecturally correct monuments. Designed to seat 1400, the auditorium of the Municipal, as with all White's theatres, was notable for its uninterrupted sight lines, fine acoustics and excellent ventilation. For him the absence of "wretched pillars" was essential so he utilised his considerable engineering skills to design a steel framed cantilever system which ensured that both circle and balcony were visibly supported by just one slender steel column. In a characteristically forthright interview published in 'The Theatre Magazine' of August 1914 White spoke of his objection to the way in which in the past theatres had been designed as if the stage was all-important but accommodation for actors too often neglected. This too he remedied in the Municipal Theatre.

Despite the extravagance of decoration in all his theatres, White was emphatic that the "three great essentials ... clear vision ... a perfect acoustic ... a scheme of ventilation ..." came first. In fact it is likely that having solved these technical problems to his own satisfaction he used pattern books as the source for his decorative embellishments. The catalogue of the first great Exhibition of Modern Decorative Arts held at Turin, Italy in 1902 was a mine of information about Art Nouveau and Jugendstil art and provided architects all over the world with details of up-to-date styles. On the exteriors of his two Brisbane theatres White had already used the swirling tendrils and sinuous stem-like forms seen first on Olbrich's Secession House, later developed and popularised at Turin by such Italian designers as Raimondo D'Aronco and Giuseppe Velati-Bellini. More restrained in Hastings, New Zealand, White nevertheless swathed the boxes on either side of the stage of the Municipal with similar motifs.

The full repertoire of Spanish Mission decoration enlivened the white plastered exterior facade of the Municipal Theatre. There are arched doors and windows, a balcony, broken columns, an ornamental balustrade, symmetrically placed long windows topped by bracketed window hoods and tiled roofed towers at each end. The Municipal Theatre, Hastings is now a building of international significance not only because of the sophistication of its construction but also because of a decorative scheme which places it in a specific period of time in the history of design.

Next door, Garnett's Municipal Building displays the same eclectic qualities which marked his 1915 designs for shops in Heretaunga Street for Kilford and Ebbett, J.Hannah and for R. Warren. None of these remains today but the surviving drawings show that the architect was devoted to the kinds of heavy projecting decorative features which were to prove so dangerous in the 1931 earthquake. These simple structures were decorated with a profusion of cornices, curved window hoods, steeped parapets and open balustrades, some classical in inspiration, others showing evidence of acquaintance with the Turin exhibition catalogue. The 1914 building known today as Credit House in Queen Street is almost certainly his work, although no plans survive to prove the matter beyond doubt.

The Municipal Building, vacated by the Council in 1977, comprised ground floor shops and a main entrance on Heretaunga Street which led to a spacious vestibule and upstairs to the Assembly Hall; the Council Chamber had a separate entrance on Eastbourne Street. In the centre of the building is a tower with tiled roof which forms a strong visual relation to the towers of the Municipal Theatre; this was used as a card room when dances were held in the Assembly Hall. At first floor level a balcony surrounds the whole structure; it projects out over the main entrance to form a space able to be used on civic ceremonial occasions.

To the architectural purist the exterior of the Municipal Building is perhaps confused, but such an eclectic approach was highly fashionable at the time it was built. In 1917 when it opened it would have appeared the height of fashion and a worthy demonstration of the town's growing commercial importance. It is thus a noteworthy survivor of a period of Hastings architecture which the earthquake all but wiped out. With the Municipal Theatre it forms a unique architectural heritage precinct which should be preserved for the future.

Garnett was responsible in 1924 for the premises known today as Poppelwell's, originally built for Fitzpatrick & Co. Its Spanish flavour derives from the overhanging cordova-tiled eaves which, like the similar one on the Municipal Theatre, dominate the upper section of the building. Here the architect used patterns in relief brickwork to contrast with the white plastered

The Municipal Theatre also functioned for many years as a cinema. This photograph was taken when Rudolph Valentino's silent movie The Sheik was screened in the early 1920's.
HAWKE'S BAY MUSEUM

25

Garnett's Villa d'Este apartments in Heretaunga Street had to be dismantled and rebuilt after the earthquake.

HAWKE'S BAY MUSEUM

Henry Eli White's Municipal Theatre, damaged but able to be restored, stands tall above the ruins of Garnett's Methodist Church opposite.

ALEXANDER TURNBULL LIBRARY
S.C.Smith Collection

facade. His elegant Villa d'Este shops and apartments, designed in 1929, were demolished following the earthquake in 1931, but later rebuilt in strengthened form to the original design.

Hastings' Spanish Mission character was firmly established before the earthquake. Even architects from outside Hastings respected the town's growing enthusiasm for the style. Wellington architects Clere and Williams were in 1920 to employ some restrained use of Spanish Mission features for their picture theatre named The Cosy, which did not survive the earthquake. So too did George Penlington, when he designed the administration block for Hastings Boys' High School in 1926. The Public Works Department in Wellington even authorised the importation of its roof tiles from Spain. Strengthening and renovation in 1979 has ensured the preservation of this notable building.

The 3rd of February 1931 was a fateful day for the whole of Hawke's Bay. That it has gone down in history as the day of "the Napier earthquake" should not detract from the fact that Hastings, with a population of 11,000, also suffered serious damage and loss of life. The swaying motion of the forces which rocked the ground in both towns had immediate effect on masonry buildings which simply crumbled. The steel reinforcing beams used in many buildings were inadequately attached to the brick walls they supported so they too collapsed. Only reinforced concrete buildings survived, most of them requiring attention as the result of cracking. Overhanging pediments, parapets and verandahs plummeted to the ground killing or seriously injuring people who rushed outside when they realised the magnitude of what was happening around them. Aftershocks which went on for some days after the main earthquake continued to weaken those buildings which had not completely collapsed already. Hastings, earlier in its history known as the Town of Blazes, was fortunate in that the fires which followed the earthquake were quickly extinguished, unlike those in Napier.

The most imposing and prominent survivor was the Hawke's Bay Farmers' Building, designed by Edmund Anscombe (1873-1948) in 1928. With W.H. Gummer and J.W. Chapman-Taylor, Anscombe is, in national terms, the most eminent architect to have worked in Hastings. Born in England he arrived in New Zealand in 1901, began his career as a builder's apprentice in Dunedin, studied architecture in the United States then returned to Dunedin in 1907 where he quickly established a flourishing practice. Following his work there on the New Zealand and South Seas Exhibition of 1925 he shifted his practice to Wellington in order to be ready to design the Centennial of New Zealand

Exhibition of 1939-40. His Hawke's Bay Farmers' Building is a three-storeyed structure built on reinforced concrete foundations with a similar superstructure. It housed a large department store on its ground floor and the town's first lift transported patrons up to a magnificently appointed tearooms and further above, to offices. Anscombe gave Hastings a building worthy of Auckland or Wellington, its first and second floor facades having the recessed windows, darkened spandrel panels and prominent pilasters of many office buildings built during the 1920s in those cities. Pilasters extend to parapet level to form rhythmical groups along the facade thus accentuating the building's height. Sadly, the interior spaces have seen frequent alteration; ceilings have been lowered and polished Tasmanian hardwood obscured, particularly on the ground floor. The original lift remains.

Sensing that this prosperous town would be likely to require his professional skills in the future, Anscombe established a branch of his Wellington practice in the Hawke's Bay Farmers' Building. The reconstruction period immediately following the earthquake was to give unexpected justification to his decision.

As Mary Boyd pointed out in her history of the town, "in rebuilding Hastings no one wanted to have anything more to do with bricks or multi-storeyed buildings." Thus St Andrew's Church lost its spire and St Matthew's had its tower considerably lowered. The Post Office, whose tower had completely collapsed, depositing its bells into the street, was temporarily restored without a tower. The Fletcher Construction Company quickly built temporary banking premises in both Hastings and Napier. James Fletcher, director of the country's largest construction firm, counselled against over hasty rebuilding and offered his services to the Prime Minister, George Forbes, in order to assist in the reconstruction. His firm, local builders H.W. Abbott and the Edwards Construction Company built many of the town's new shops, often, as Fletcher pointed out, making no profit whatever.

The bulk of the architectural work was done by an association of architects formed, as at Napier, across normal professional boundaries, to see to the efficient replacement of damaged premises. Among its Hastings members were the firms of Davies, Garnett and Phillips; Edmund Anscombe and Associates and other architects from Napier, Wellington and Auckland.

Initially the work involved the demolition of wrecked buildings and the carrying out of essential repairs to damaged ones. It was not until 1933-34 that substantial numbers of new buildings began to appear fully completed in the town's central business district. As at nearby Napier architects tended to design

The interior of the Tea Rooms in the Hawke's Bay Farmers' Building, Hastings, reproduced from MODERN ARCHITECTURAL SERVICE as Practiced by Edmund Anscombe and Associates.
THE CLIFF PRESS, HASTINGS 1934

The bells of the Post Office tower were deposited unceremoniously on to Queen Street during the earthquake.
ALEXANDER TURNBULL LIBRARY

The single-storeyed Westerman & Co. building of 1921 had to be completely demolished after the earthquake.
ALEXANDER TURNBULL LIBRARY
S.C.Smith Collection

Dislodged columns inside Westerman's show the extent of the structural damage.
ALEXANDER TURNBULL LIBRARY
E.Pickering Donation

fairly conventional office and business premises whose distinguishing factor was the exterior use of Spanish Mission or Art Deco styling. It is this more than anything else which has made both towns internationally known among enthusiasts for 1930s architecture. Hastings has a pedigree of Spanish Mission buildings which pre-dates the 1931 earthquake. It is significant that Hastings also has a number of fine Art Deco buildings equally as interesting as those in Napier though perhaps less unified in scale and location.

The most immediately arresting of the new Hastings commercial premises was the department store Anscombe designed for Westerman & Co in 1932. Like all other post-earthquake buildings it was built entirely of reinforced concrete with the exception of one cavity brick wall. The architect seized the opportunity of a highly visible site at the corner of Russell and Heretaunga Streets to add something of his own to the Spanish Mission character of Hastings. Westerman's, established in 1910, was one of the town's oldest firms. The company's 1921 building on the same site had been completely destroyed in the earthquake but fortunately many of its interior fittings, including a magnificent wooden staircase designed by Albert Garnett, were able to be re-used in the new building.

Anscombe divided the longer Russell Street elevation into three sections along which he used a number of highly characterful Spanish Mission features. On the shorter Heretaunga Street elevation he flanked a group of three round-headed windows with a pair of square-headed ones capped with decorative mouldings. The splayed corner at the centre links the two elevations, drawing attention to its importance by means of a pair of French doors which give on to a balcony with a wrought iron balustrade. The doorway is framed with barley twist half columns and fluted Corinthian pilasters. The round-headed fanlight over the doors is framed by an elaborately moulded arch which is echoed in the frieze decoration above. A verandah with a highly embossed pressed metal ceiling is wrapped around both facades; the use of decorative lead lights in the glazing below is particularly impressive.

During the 1980s Westerman's was ill-used by various tenants who, failing to acknowledge the building's special character, covered its facades with unsympathetic signs. In 1991 an auction of the old shop's 1921 interior fittings passed them off to an unsuspecting public as Art Deco! Some of these have now found their way into a wine bar which, if not the ideal place to house elegant wooden fittings originally designed to display such things as women's frocks and furs, at least guarantees their survival in Hastings.

Anscombe's sympathetic restoration of the severely damaged buildings at

Iona at Havelock North ensured that the Spanish Mission character which Rush gave them as far back as 1911 remained for the future. The buildings Anscombe designed in restrained Art Deco or stripped classical styles: Kershaw's and the State Theatre (in association with the Auckland architect Vernon Brown) in 1933, the Central Building in 1934 and the Dominion Restaurant in 1935 were obviously not commissioned by clients with large budgets. Such was not the case when in 1934 the architect was employed to build a large single-storeyed homestead at Washpool, another large land holding on what was formerly part of the Maraekakaho Station.

Mrs Esmé Glazebrook had been a pupil at Iona; she was familiar with Tauroa, Arden and Te Mata, houses on which W.H. Gummer had allowed his familiarity with Californian Spanish influence to be displayed. The client decided to commission Edmund Anscombe, working in nearby Hastings, to design a house which, as Westerman had done, made use of the fully stylistic armoury of Spanish Mission. The house is a clever manipulation of an established architectural vocabulary, in a way none of Gummer's ever was.

It was built around a four-roomed cottage whose proportions were hugely extended. A long garden front elevation is dominated by a projecting bay with curved parapet and a group of three fan-lit round-headed windows separated by barley twist columns. To one side is an arcaded verandah with three openings. Angled cordova tiles and blind balustrading break the parapet line. Inside rooms are proportioned on a grand scale, many of them with elaborately moulded cornices and picture panels. Washpool is also justly celebrated for its magnificent gardens based on designs prepared in 1935 by the Christchurch firm of landscape gardeners, A.W. Buxton and Sons.

In central Hastings the enthusiasm for Spanish Mission building continued. Next door to Westerman & Co on Russell Street, Harvey's, the firm of hardware and china importers, had impressive new Spanish-styled premises designed by Albert Garnett. An unusual feature of the interior of the shop is a central staircase ascending to a balconied first floor; this detail is said to have had its origin in Mr H.G. Harvey's enthusiasm for the department stores he visited in Paris during the First World War. When the shop was officially opened in time for Christmas 1933, customers were given copies of a commemorative brochure with an introduction in Maori and illustrated with drawings by Colin Wilkinson.

Because of their shared architectural character Westerman's, Harvey's, Christie's and Swan and Lavalle's CML Building, which completes the group at the end of Russell Street, are the most important commercial buildings in Hastings' Spanish Mission cityscape. In 1988 this architectural character was

At the opening in 1933 of Nathan & Co's building, tenants and construction workers assembled for a commemorative photograph. Why some of those pictured are wearing false noses remains a mystery!
ALEXANDER TURNBULL LIBRARY
Whitehead Collection

Colin Wilkinson's illustrations of the exterior and interior of Harvey's were reproduced in the commemorative brochure issued for the shop's re-opening in 1933.

HARVEY FAMILY

correctly identified as significant both in terms of the city's central business district and its surrounding area. As a result, in consultation with Beca, Carter, Hollings & Ferner, the Hastings District Council decided to promote a Spanish Mission theme in order to encourage the re-development of older buildings in the centre of the city.

In an example of foresighted urban planning which could well be emulated in other towns and cities in New Zealand, the Council did extensive historical research and in 1990 published comprehensive architectural guidelines in draft form. Its intention and eventual effect was to encourage the owners of businesses to identify their buildings correctly, thereby ensuring that both painting and signage were carried out in sympathy with the individual building's architectural character within the context of the cityscape. The Council led the way with a public amenity building programme which showed how the choice of a Spanish Mission architectural design theme and use of appropriate materials could contribute significantly to rather than detract from the city's already distinctive architectural character.

Other architectural practices in Hastings preferred to decorate their otherwise modest buildings with Art Deco motifs. Davies and Phillips, the surviving members of a busy practice which had for many years numbered Albert Garnett among its partners, was Hastings' best known practice in the three decades following the earthquake. Its principal was Harold Davies (1886-1976) who as early as 1916 had designed an extraordinary Baptist Church for Hastings two years after having moved there from Wellington. The other partner was Hastings-born Eric Phillips (1897-1980), who had been employed by Hoggard, Prouse and Gummer in its Wellington office from 1914 and supervised the building of Tauroa for Gummer in 1915-16. Following service overseas during the First World War he completed the examinations for an associateship of the Royal Institute of British Architects in London and then returned to work in Gummer's Auckland office. In 1920 he joined Henry Hyland and Harold Davies in partnership and in 1924 won a national competition with his design for Napier's magnificent Public Trust Building. By 1936 the Hastings firm was known as Davies and Phillips, changing its name to include that of Sidney Chaplin after World War II when the young man who had served his articles there, returned. It was Harold Davies who had arranged that Chaplin spend the year 1925 as a junior draughtsman at Gummer and Ford's Auckland office.

Both Harold Davies and Eric Phillips contributed modestly to the Spanish character of Hastings architecture; their Hastings Methodist Church of 1931-2 situated opposite the Municipal Theatre adds considerably to the Spanish flavour of this particular area of the city. Their Iona Chapel of 1957 is a belated though undeniably accomplished addition to the tradition. Although Harold Davies designed a large house in Spanish Mission idiom in 1935 for the builder H.W. Abbott, it was never built.

In the 1930s Davies and Phillips were the chief exponents of Art Deco in Hastings. Their Heretaunga Buildings, a 1935 reconstruction of the 1922 classically detailed original building by Hyland and Phillips, is typical of their work. As 'Home and Building' informed its national readership in November 1937, the two ground floor shopfronts, House of Blackmore, a mens' outfitters, and Alan Grant, Chemist, "offered considerable scope to the designer, and the materials involved—Glass, chromium-plated metal, tiles or terrazzo—are capable of manipulation into a variety of interesting forms." Sidney Chaplin's 1938 premises for John Hill Ltd and the former Dental and Medical Chambers, now Commercial Union Insurance, of 1935 designed by Davies and Phillips, also proved how enduring the smart Art Deco styling was. So too did their Crematorium in 1945.

Garnett too, although no longer part of the partnership, designed the impressive Art Deco Carlsson Flats in 1933 and, in 1934 Holden's Building. Still active during the 1940s he was frequently called upon to design what can best be described as Spanish Deco houses which combined the pared back Moderne house with all the decorative details commonly found on Spanish Mission buildings.

In other buildings such as the 1932 Queen's Chambers and the Commercial Bank of Australia (now Williams and Kettle) and the 1935 Karamu Chambers (now Esam Cushing & Co), Davies and Phillips designed modest two-storeyed buildings with a rounded corner, set-back windows and stripped classical rather than Art Deco detailing. The Government Architect J.T. Mair's 1932 Post Office exhibited the same restraint which was obviously considered more respectable for banks, government and legal offices and doctors' premises. In 1925 a precedent for this had already been set by Wellington architect Stanley Fearn's Public Trust building with its superbly detailed entry dominated by two double height Ionic columns.

S.G. Chaplin did not become a partner of Davies and Phillips until after World War II. In 1934 it was decided in Hastings to call for competitive designs for a town clock to be situated at the railway crossing in Heretaunga Street. The judges of the competition were to be Harold Davis and Eric Phillips. After a lengthy correspondence with W.H. Gummer, at that time President of the New

The premises of Alan Grant, Chemist, and the House of Blackmore, tenants of Heretaunga Chambers, were dressed in the fashionable Art Deco manner by Davies and Phillips in 1935.
HOME AND BUILDING, NOVEMBER 1937

Queen's Chambers (1932) by Davies and Phillips.
ALEXANDER TURNBULL LIBRARY
Whitehead Collection

The Commercial Bank of Australia Building, also by
Davies and Phillips (1932).
ALEXANDER TURNBULL LIBRARY
Whitehead Collection

This floral model of the Town Clock was made for the
Hastings Blossom Festival of 1956.
ALEXANDER TURNBULL LIBRARY

Zeland Institute of Architects, on the dangers of demeaning competitions by offering inadequate prize money, S.G. Chaplin was awarded the first prize of 25 guineas. The clocktower was built in 1935 and it incorporated a new clock and the chimes from John Campbell's 1909 Post Office which the earthquake had fatally weakened.

In the late 1980s the square near the clocktower was the subject of extensive improvements made according to the Hastings District Council's Spanish Mission development theme. It is now dominated by a large water feature which blends well with the two-storeyed Spanish Mission buildings nearby on Russell Street. The 1989 amenity block opposite Poppelwell's features a painted roughcast surface, sloping brick corner buttresses, tiled roof and tower with curved parapet, overhanging eaves lined with exposed rafters and a cleverly conceived system of brick-outlined blind arcading.

By promoting the philosophy that additions of any kind to a building should always be thought of as part of the building and those around it, rather than merely an unrelated object, the Hastings district Council's Spanish Mission theme will eventually result in Hastings being able to boast an appearance which acknowledges the existence of an architectural tradition going back many decades.

In recognition of the far sighted planning and design achievement for the city's central business district, the Hastings District Council and Beca Carter Hollings & Ferner received the New Zealand Planning Institute's 1991 Award of Merit. The award also recognised the physical changes which had been made in central Hastings; the pedestrianisation of a section of Heretaunga Street, the use of water to link the two halves of the street formerly separated by the railway line, traffic diversions and the encouragement of a Spanish Mission architectural theme.

New Zealand can ill afford to neglect its architectural past. In Hastings, a city where some of the country's finest architects worked, local body politicians have realised that this heritage must be nurtured and that awareness of history is not destructive of progress.

The Church of the Sacred Heart (1895) by Sollitt and Allan
still dominates the skyline of Hastings. The timber work of
this soaring Gothic structure is characteristic of George
Sollitt's Victorian architecture.

Horonui (1899-1900) by George Sollitt is an extended single
storeyed villa with a verandah along its garden front.

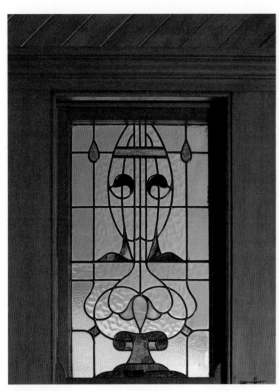

Horonui's billiard room is notable for its rimu-panelled, coved ceiling and stained glass.

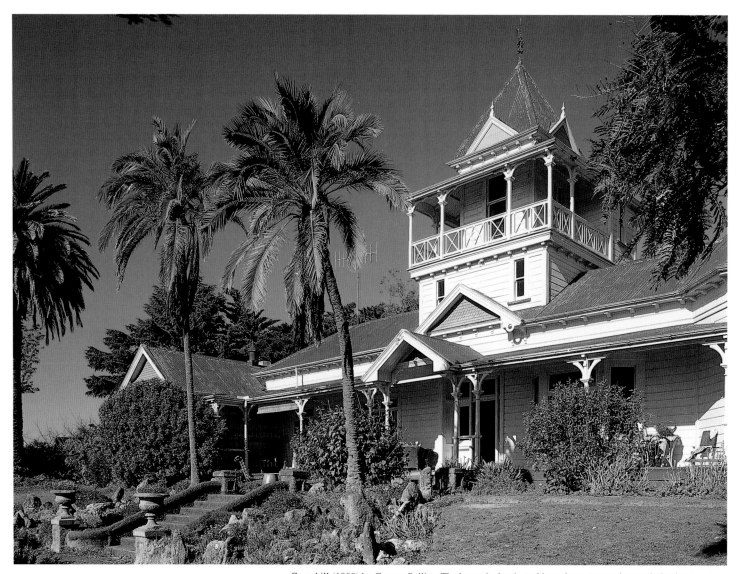

Greenhill (1900) by George Sollitt. The house is dominated by a three-storeyed central viewing tower to enable the occupants to survey the Ngatarawa Plain below.

Glazed panel above an interior door.

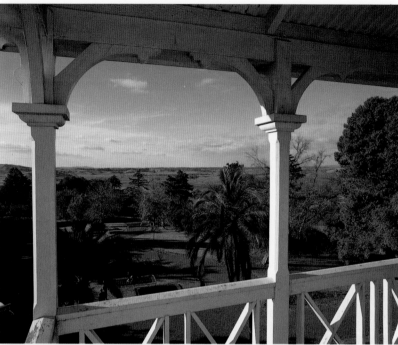

Part of the extensive view from the tower.

Hand-painted stained glass door panels at Greenhill depict English pastoral scenes.

Paired posts support the verandah.

Matapiro (1902-1910) by C.T. Natusch was built in stages around a smaller original house. Its symmetrical garden facade dominated by half-timbered gables hides the complexity of the plan which is visible from the rear.

The magnificent panelled hall and dining room are connected by a folding door. Above the stair landing is an example of Art Nouveau glass so fashionable in the first decade of the century.

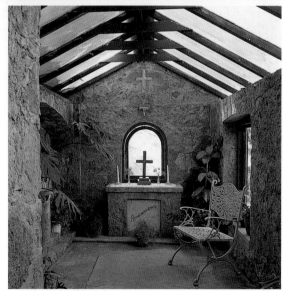

Called the Little Church of the Flowers, the grotto-chapel at Matapiro commemorates Walter Shrimpton for whom the house was built.

Tuna Nui (1912) by Natusch and Frankland. Exterior walls of two-inch thick stucco and a tiled roof give this house an unusual appearance for its time.

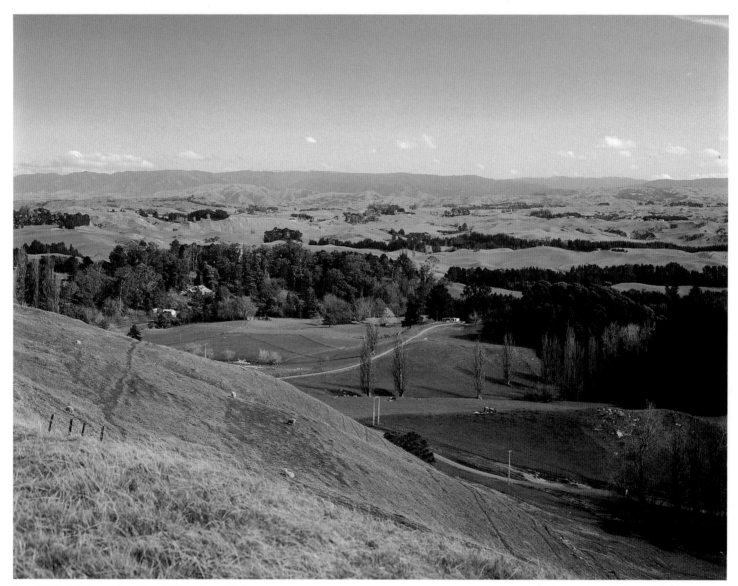

Tuna Nui in its hill country setting at Sherenden, with the ranges
in the distance.

The Anglican Church of St Matthew (1886) by C.J. Mountfort was extended in 1914 by the Wellington architect Frederick de Jersey Clere. Although it demonstrates the architect's advocacy of such modern materials as ferro-concrete and his adherence to Gothic principles, the result of the union with Mountfort's wooden church is unusual despite attempts to unify the building's disparate sections with paint. It is approached by an unusual cloister.

Inside, the concrete construction is clearly visible on the chancel's coffered, barrel-vaulted ceiling.

Among the chief glories of St Matthew's are the windows in the Lady Chapel, the work of the eminent English stained glass artist Karl Parsons. In 1914 he designed the five-light Adoration of the Blessed Virgin with Christ, Shepherds and the Magi.

Parsons added three smaller windows in 1926: the Virgin Annunciate; The Archangel Gabriel with the Annunciation below; St Joseph with the Flight into Egypt below. These are renowned for the intensity of their colour.

Mudgway House, Duke Street, Hastings (1913) by Grant and Ball. One of Hastings' grandest single-storeyed villas, this house has an elaborate return verandah and entry porch.

Kopanga (1912) by J.A. Louis Hay. Unlike other large houses by the architect this huge concrete house survived the earthquake in 1931. The garden and drive were laid out by the Christchurch landscape gardening firm of A.W. Buxton and Sons who frequently achieved commissions from wealthy landed Hawke's Bay families.

In 1910 Hay designed the smaller "Mens'Whare," and then began work on Kopanga which was not complete until 1914.

St Luke's Church, Havelock North (1912) and the Village Hall, Havelock North (1911), both by W.J. Rush.

Ngawiwi (1909), the house Rush designed for himself in Havelock North.

McHardy House, Havelock North (1916) also by W.J. Rush. Sleeping verandahs were an essential feature of the architect's Havelock houses.

Woodford House (1911) by W.J. Rush

The Quadrangle, Woodford House with Davies and Phillips'
Holland House (1934) at the rear.

Chapel of St Francis of Assisi, Woodford House, (1927) by
Clere and Clere. In 1968 the chapel was sympathetically
enlarged by Wylde-Brown and Roberts.

Iona, Havelock North (1913) by W.J. Rush was the earliest and largest Spanish Mission-influenced building in the district.

Iona Chapel (1957) by Davies and Phillips continued the Spanish theme.

Whare Ra (1913) by J.W. Chapman-Taylor, built as the home of Dr Robert Felkin, founder of the Order of the Golden Dawn in New Zealand.

The concrete rear elevation of Whare Ra houses the Temple of the Golden Dawn.

In this elaborately painted seven-sided vault members of the Order spent whole nights in meditation.

Oak Trees (1919) by J.W. Chapman-Taylor was built as a temporary dwelling while the architect was working on Sunborne (1920), his first concrete house on the section above.

Inside Sunborne the architect's talent for creating intimate spaces is evident. The dark stained, hand-adzed rimu beams are also characteristic of his respect for craftsmanship.

The unusual bath is made of coloured tiles laid on concrete.

Tauroa (1916) by W.H. Gummer.

Tauroa's gates, entry and double curving stairwell indicate why this house is renowned for its craftsmanship as well as its superb design. The inscription in beaten copper on the fire hood is similar to others in houses belonging to members of the Order of the Golden Dawn.

The side elevation of Tauroa with Georgian shuttered windows and Spanish Mission bell aperture set into the parapet.

Craggy Range (now known as Belmount) (1918-19) by W.H. Gummer.
The north-east facing elevation displays the house's extraordinary modernity.

Gummer's garden elevation is less successfully handled. The long garden
wall is connected to the house and features elegantly sloping corner
buttresses.

Craggy Range seen in its rural setting across the Tukituki River. Alongside, part of the buttressed garden wall and the entrance gates which reflect the character of the house.

Arden (1926) by Gummer and Ford shows the architects' familiarity with the Spanish Modern domestic architecture of California.

The side elevation shows Gummer's porte cochère which was added in 1985.

This motif in the balustrade of the staircase is repeated in the exterior detailing.

An external stair leads up to the roof on which it was originally intended to build a swimming pool.

Arden's Juliet balcony.

Te Mata (1935) by Gummer and Ford. The architects favoured a simpler Spanish-Georgian composition when they replaced the overbearingly Spanish-styled house which W.J. Rush had designed in 1920 and which collapsed in the 1931 earthquake. All that survives of Rush's work are the architect's watercolour elevations and the brick garden walls.

·RESIDENCE· TE· MATA·
·FOR·BERNARD· CHAMBERS· ESQ·
· SCALE · 8 · FT · TO · ONE · INCH ·
· SHEET · 3 ·

·SOUTH· ELEVATION·

·EAST· ELEVATION·

·NORTH· ELEVATION·

·WEST· ELEVATION·

W· J· RUSH· F· N· Z· I· A·
REGD· ARCHITECT·

Typical houses by W. J. Rush (above left) which show the enduring popularity of large two-storeyed English homes among Hastings wealthier citizens.

Beatson House (1914) by Albert Garnett (lower left) shows how carefully the Architect had absorbed the work of English domestic architects, despite his provision of distinctly antipodean sleeping verandahs.

The Cato House (1914-15) called St. Brigid's (above) is the work of an unknown English architect whose design the client had seen in a magazine and had replicated in Hastings. The sun-trap plan was frequently used by Chapman-Taylor but by few other New Zealand architects.

Baird House (1924) by Davies, Hyland & Phillips (right) which again shows extensive sleeping verandahs.

Glen Aros (1914) and Torran (1911) were designed by Albert Garnett in a Californian bungalow style.

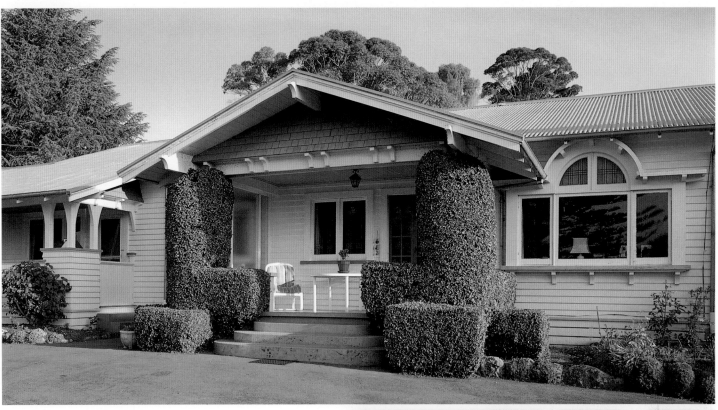

Also by Garnett is Glenalvon (1927) whose cedar-planted drive is another of those laid out by A.W. Buxton and Sons.

The Municipal Theatre, Hastings (1914) by Henry Eli White boasts the city's most impressive Spanish Mission frontage and ornate interior decoration.

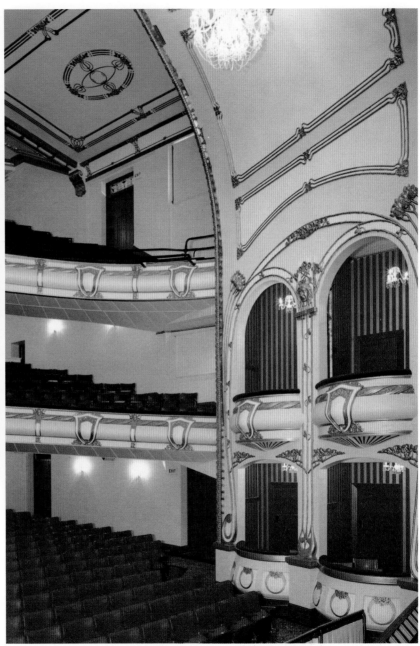

The boxes on either side of the stage are decorated with floral motifs
similar to those used by architects of the Austrian Secession.

Municipal Building, Hastings (1915) by Albert Garnett (above left) with the Municipal Theatre beside.

Hawke's Bay Farmers' Building (1928) by Edmund Anscombe and Associates (left).   Built in reinforced concrete, it was a notable earthquake survivor.

Credit House (1914) (left) is probably Garnett's work too.

Hastings Boys' High School's Frank Crist Building (1926) by George Penlington   (above right) continues the Spanish theme with its curved parapets and bracketed eaves supporting a tiled roof.

Public Trust (1925) by Stanley Fearn (right) displays the classicism considered suitable for public institutions.

Villa D'Este (1929) shops and apartments by Albert Garnett (centre right).

Poppelwell's (1924), originally premises of Fitzpatrick & Co by Albert Garnett (bottom right). The Spanish idiom is clearly recognisable.

Westerman & Co. (1932)   Edmund Anscombe and Associates.
In replacing the collapsed 1921 premises of the company Anscombe revived the town's Spanish Mission architectural theme. Here the barley twist columns, round-headed windows and balconies are combined with classically derived details.

Westerman's verandah has a pressed metal ceiling and a variety of windows in stained and clear glass. The building's interior wooden fittings survived from the original 1921 shop. The staircase was built to a design by Albert Garnett.

Kershaw's (1933) and the Dominion Restaurant (1935) were both designed by Edmund Anscombe and Associates in a restrained Art Deco style. The State Theatre (1933) was designed by Anscombe and the Auckland architect Vernon Brown in association. Both architectural students and established practitioners were keen to take advantage of post-earthquake work opportunities in Hawke's Bay.

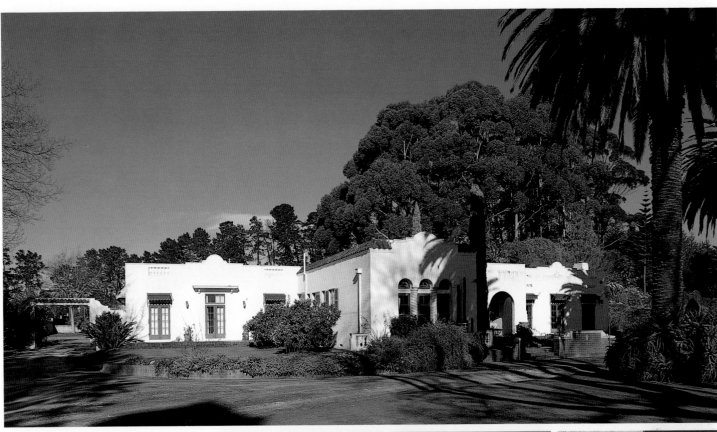

Washpool (1934) by Edmund Anscombe. This is one of New Zealand's largest Spanish-styled houses.

Anscombe's exterior detailing is impeccable although inside he reverted to an acceptable Georgian plan with classically-derived decorative treatment of cornices and supporting brackets.

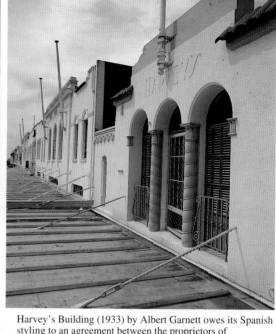

Harvey's Building (1933) by Albert Garnett owes its Spanish styling to an agreement between the proprietors of Westerman's and Harvey's that their adjoining buildings should share an architectural character—hence the sloping cordova tiles, group of round-headed windows, barley twist columns and decorative railings. The only exception was Harvey's Art Deco glass lay light.

The Russell Street Spanish precinct concludes with Swan and Lavalle's 1929 Colonial Mutual Life Building, now Minh Ta Design.

Hastings Methodist Church (1931-2) by Davies and Phillips picks up the Spanish theme from its position opposite the Municipal Theatre.

St Andrew's Hall (1935). Although its architect is not known, whoever was responsible was familiar with the Spanish Mission and Art Deco character of the newly restored town after 1931.

The Commercial Union Insurance building was originally built as Dental and Medical Chambers in 1935 by Davies and Phillips. Its streamlined rounded corners, metal windows, projecting upper window and decorative outlining of edges can be seen on the same practice's Crematorium (1945).

John Hill Electrical (1938) is the work of S.G. Chaplin. Corner-sited buildings made much of the rounded edges characteristic of Art Deco architecture.

Heretaunga Chambers (1935) and the Hawke's Bay Electric Power Board were both designed by Davies and Phillips, the latter a reconstruction of Hyland and Phillips' 1922 stripped classical building. The new version replaced classical detailing with Art Deco motifs.

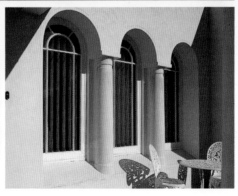

Garnett's personal contribution to post earthquake housing was a blend of Spanish Mission with Moderne—Spanish Deco. The houses were all built during the early 1940s but Gloucester House (demolished in 1990) dates from 1935.

In 1935 Harold Davies of Davies and Phillips designed this large Spanish-styled house for the Hastings builder H.W. Abbott. It was never built.

Holden's Building (1934) by Albert Garnett with its corner known as Nutter's and the premises of Williams and Kettle formerly the Commercial Bank of Australia (1932) by Davies and Phillips are fine examples of New Zealand 1930s Art Deco and stripped classical buildings whose painted appearance today obscures their architectural character. The Hastings District Council is vigorously promoting guidelines for decoration and signage which will restore such buildings to their full glory.

Hastings Post Office was designed by the Government Architect, J.T. Mair in 1932. Like the Public Trust this large public building was designed in a more severe stripped classical style.

Carlsson Flats (1933) by Albert Garnett is one of the city's most accomplished Art Deco buildings.

77

Built with appropriate style and materials, the amenity block and ornamental garden in the town centre were completed in 1989 as part of the Spanish Mission architectural theme promoted by the Hastings District Council.

Hastings Clock Tower (1934) by S.G. Chaplin. In this concrete tower hang the bells which were formerly housed in the Post Office tower which collapsed in 1931.

BIBLIOGRAPHY

Boyd, M.B. **City of the Plains—A History of Hastings.**
Victoria University Press for Hastings City Council 1984

Grant, S.W. **Havelock North from Village to Borough 1860-1952.**
Hawke's Bay Newspapers Ltd 1978

Grant S.W. **In Other Days—A History of the Chambers Family of Te Mata.**
Central Hawke's Bay Printers and Publishers, Waipukurau 1980.

McGregor, Robert. **The Great Quake.**
Regional Publications Ltd, Napier 1989

Morrison, Robin. **Images of a House.**
Alister Taylor 1978

Shaw, Peter and Hallett, Peter. **Art Deco Napier—Styles of the Thirties.**
Reed Methuen 1987, Second Edition—Cosmos Publications 1990

Shaw, Peter. **New Zealand Architecture from Polynesian Beginnings to 1990.**
Hodder and Stoughton 1991.

Tipples, Rupert. **Colonial Landscape Gardener—Alfred Buxton of Christchurch, New Zealand 1872-1950.**
Department of Horticulture and Landscape, Lincoln College, Canterbury 1989.

Weitze, Karen J. **California's Mission Revival.**
Hennessey and Ingalls, Inc., Los Angeles 1984.

Hawkes Bay "Before" and "After" The Great Earthquake of 1931.
Daily Telegraph Co Ltd, Napier 1981.